How to ~~Write a Novel in 20 Steps~~

If you are looking for a process to start writing a novel or tips to write a better novel, this book is great place to start.

This book contains the lessons learned by attorney and author Adam Van Susteren to help you start and finish a better novel in twenty steps.

Novels by Adam Van Susteren:

<u>The Aaron Baker Series:</u>
Wounded By Her Guardian
Sunshine or Lead
The Dinosaur Lawyer

<u>The Jo Channing Series:</u>
Blanket Immunity
Gangster's Court (coming soon)

FOREWORD

Writing is a craft. The challenge: to take the story that's in your head, with all its sights, sounds, smells, and feelings and immerse readers in it by only using words. The goal: for the reader to love the story to the point where they can't help but ask *what happens next?* This book will help you write a novel where readers want to know what happens next.

I've run a beta writers group in San Diego since 2013 and have read over 200 different authors' words in that group. Most writers come to the group looking for validation, that their writing is the best anyone has ever read. Without exception, all writers initial foray into the beta writing group show they need work to produce their best writing.

I met Adam Van Susteren when he joined my group a few years ago. He was introduced to the "words on paper" concept and his craft improved tremendously. He has taken everything he learned from writing his first four novels and in our group to create something special with this how-to book.

In this book, he breaks down the Herculean task of writing a novel into twenty manageable steps and provides easy to understand examples. The lessons herein will help writers not only start writing a novel but also improve their craft.

Whether you've got an idea in your head for your first novel, have completed a manuscript, or have self-published a few novels, I can promise this book will not only help you actually write a novel - it will help you write a better novel.

David S. Larson
www.DavidSLarson.com

TABLE OF CONTENTS

Five Parts of the Novelist's Path

Steps to Writing Your Novel

HOW TO WRITE A NOVEL IN 20 STEPS

BY

ADAM VAN SUSTEREN

FIVE PARTS OF THE NOVELIST'S PATH

I. WRITE

Find time to get in front of a computer or notepad and write. Your goal is to find ways to make sure you write when the words are flowing and try to keep the clogs from stopping you.

Something I found effective was joining a weekly writing group where you submit a chapter each week for another writer to review your submission and, in turn, you review a chapter of theirs. Try to find a writers group in your area on Meetup.com, Craigslist, Facebook, or by doing a Google search. Deadlines and peer pressure are incredibly effective motivators.

Even with someone excited for your next submission, invariably, at some point, you will be stuck. Try skipping ahead in the story to something you think will be fun to write. Maybe a chase scene or confrontation. Maybe something with a lot of dialogue – anything to encourage you to keep writing your novel.

If you find you just need a break from the entire project, instead of allowing yourself to sit in a corner and hate the process, I suggest you take a break to read a book. Don't watch television during this break. Read a book from start to finish. When you finish reading, hopefully you'll be full of fresh ideas for what you can do in your story and be reminded of how amazing a novel is.

II.   READ

If you're not an avid reader before deciding to write your first book, you are at a disadvantage. Reading good books will help you understand plot developments, character arcs, effective dialogue, etc. Even reading bad books will also help you understand how important it is to have good plot developments, character arcs, effective dialogue, etc.

I cannot emphasize enough – read. If you are going to write a young adult book, read *Twilight*. If you want to write a mystery, read *Sherlock Holmes*. And then go to Amazon and find something else in the genre with bad reviews and read it, or at least the part of it that has a free preview. Read not only to enjoy the book, but also to understand the difference between a book that sells millions of copies and one that few people start but rarely finish. Best-sellers do a lot right with their story, learn from them. Non-sellers do a lot wrong with their story, learn from them.

Your goal in writing a novel is to sell it, right? Reading books will help you understand your competition. You can't expect to succeed without looking to learn from the success and failure of others on the same path.

Reading a few books before and during the writing process will help you write a better novel.

III.   REVIEW

You should find other aspiring authors and trade chapter reviews as you work on your novel. If you can't find a group on Meetup.com, Craigslist, Facebook, etc., go to Amazon and search for authors in your genre who have few reviews; odds are they are working on their next novel and would be willing to trade chapter-for-chapter reviews with you.

When you review someone else's work, it gets you thinking of what's good and what could be better for your own story. If your writing has lots of point of view shifts, verb tense issues, or pacing problems, but you don't notice, you might see your own error when you review someone else's work.

When you have reviewed and critiqued someone else's work, you can better understand how it isn't personal when you receive painful feedback. By reviewing the work of others, you will be better prepared to have your own work reviewed, which will help you write a better novel.

In addition to finding someone else's work to edit, write reviews for books you've read on Amazon, Barnes & Noble, Goodreads, and other places. After spending ten hours reading a book, what are the big takeaways? What was good? What was bad? What kept your interest or lost it? Writing a good review is difficult, but it can also be a great exercise to help hone your skills as a writer. The most important piece of writing in your novel is on your back cover. Your summary of the book must give enough information to hook the reader, but not so much that it gives away the plot. If you've practiced this skill by writing a dozen reviews, you will be much sharper when it's time to write your back cover.

Learning to effectively critique great, good, okay, and bad writing will help you write a better novel.

IV.   EDIT

My friend, author Travis Lee, reminded me of the
Hemingway quote, "The first draft of anything is shit." For
me, and most, editing is the hardest part of the writing
process.

While Hemingway focuses on the back end, I focus on the
beginning and liken writing to cooking a giant feast. Your first
draft is on the table, you want to enjoy it, but everyone who
reads your book is pointing out how you could have made the
meal better. It feels personal. It hurts. And it hurts so much
because the criticism is probably sound.

Sound advice in the kitchen is to taste as you go. This is
even more important for writing. If you review your work as
you build on it, it will make a final edit much easier. First, you
will have cleaned up a lot of mistakes. Second, and maybe
even more importantly, you will have learned how to deal with
criticism and keep going. Would you rather hear your broth is
too salty before or after you added all your meat and
vegetables? Before. Because you can taste it, re-taste it, then
decide if you want to keep it as is or alter it. Same with your
novel.

Let's say your story involves a murder by poison. You
have a pharmacist read your book and they tell you that the
poison you used doesn't work in the way it was portrayed. Or,
someone tells you a gun doesn't work as described. Or, a lead
character is so unlikeable that the story is hard to read. It's
better to have a taste of the problem as you go. That way, if
you so decide, you can change the poison, gun, or character
trait at the beginning of the story. You will find this to be a lot
easier than waiting until after you're close to the finish line to
make the changes.

Edit your own work before handing it to someone else.
That starts with running spell-check and continues with

reading it aloud in some parts. Hearing your writing out loud makes it sound much different than how it reads in your head. As writers, we know the background, the future, everything about our story – the reader only knows what they've read. Our brains autocorrect our writing for it to make sense to us, but the reader will be left out in the cold. This is why it is so important to get others to read your writing.

While you are ultimately responsible for your book, you need, yes need, to have other people review and edit your book along the way. Give people small chunks, about 2500 words at a time, so they aren't overwhelmed with having to edit an entire book.

Waiting until the end to edit is too late. A great story can die because of plot holes, poorly written passages, logic bombs, or unlikeable characters; and it is nearly impossible to properly diffuse plot problems after the entire story is written.

You need other people to read your writing along the way. I strongly suggest an exchange with another writer, but if you have a large budget you can hire a professional editor and have them edit as you write.

V.   MARKET

It is incredibly important to understand that you will be primarily responsible for marketing your novel, especially in the beginning of your writing career. Even John Grisham and James Patterson post about their novels on their Instagram accounts (or someone does it for them). You need to build your own marketing platform, even if you aim to land an agent.

It is difficult to find a literary agent. If you can show you have a built-in following, agents will be more interested in representing someone with thousands of contacts than someone with only a few. So regardless of whether you try to find an agent or choose to self-publish, building a network of people who will read your book is crucial to success.

Your ultimate goal is to get your book into the hands of readers. That can be done with a big publisher, small publisher, or self-publishing. The whole publishing world is in flux right now. It's uncertain how it will look ten years from now, but what is certain, well-written stories will always be in demand.

When you have your well-written story, you'll need a marketing plan. And just like it is with editing, it will be beneficial to constantly build as you go. Establish a social media presence. Enter writing contests for segments of your novel as well as your full manuscript. Take steps to build your brand as an author of an entertaining and well-written novel.

STEPS TO WRITING YOUR NOVEL

1. Find Your Idea

Your novel starts with an idea for a story. If you already have your idea – robots take over the world, girl falls in love with boy, office worker becomes hero, etc., then you can skip this step and go straight to turning it into a plot. If you want help coming up with your idea, keep reading this step.

I'm not terribly creative. I was a member of a legal organization for ten years before starting my first novel. I thought *what if* – about the organization. *What if* this group that has a lot of powerful people makes an unsuspecting attorney expose a governmental conspiracy involving the United States Dollar. That was the idea I turned into a novel.

Your idea for your novel should be something that interests you. If you're in sales and love sales, a novel about a salesperson needing to make a sale to pay for a surgery for a sick child would be a fine idea. If you know nothing about sales, and don't want to learn about it, having a salesperson as a main character going through your plot is a bad idea. If you love physics and want to learn about quantum mechanics, writing about a student who must invent the widget to save the world would be a good idea.

You don't have to be a doctor to write a medical thriller, a cop to write a murder mystery, or a lawyer to write a legal drama – but you want to research so you are knowledgeable about whatever topic you're writing.

If you want to create a fantasy world, like Harry Potter, Game of Thrones, or Hunger Games – that's fantastic. Just remember you still need an idea for the story you tell in the world you create.

If you're having trouble coming up with your idea, play the *what if* game about something you know a lot about, want to learn more about, or find interesting. Here's my sample idea that we'll use to build on and walk through the rest of the steps.

I've got an idea – what if people who buy *How to Write a Novel in 20 Steps* are identified as free thinkers by the government and targeted for termination. We now have a general idea. We need to turn the idea into a plot.

We need a protagonist (hero), antagonist (villain), inciting incident, climax, resolution, and secondary characters. Plugging those into your idea is your novel!

We start by plotting it out.

2. Figure Out Your Plot

Technically, the plot is nothing more than the series of events in your story. In reality, the plot is the purpose of your story, the reason it starts and ends, and what keeps a readers' attention. There is a simple formula for your plot and subplots.

- Inciting incident
- Tension and valleys
- Climax
- Resolution

The inciting incident—a body falls from the sky. Tension—the person who finds it is suspected of the murder. Climax—as the cuffs are being slapped on, another body falls from the sky. Resolution—the cop agrees not to arrest the hero but to work with her to find the reason for bodies falling from the sky. That is another inciting incident. We again build tension in valleys until the story peaks at a climax, then resolve it. Repeat.

While we have a series of many events, our main plot is the final resolution, stopping bodies from falling from the sky, which was the issue raised in our initial inciting event.

You can turn your idea into a plot, an organized series of events, any way you'd like. After settling on my idea, I like to start by thinking of my protagonist. It helps me know who will be leading the reader through the story. Let's say our protagonist is Pro, a seventeen-year-old boy who wants to write a novel to impress a girl, Crush, in his creative writing class.

Next, I like to think about the inciting incident. Regardless of genre, we want a gripping event. Let's make our inciting incident a seemingly random school shooting, where Pro hides with Crush in a supply closet and overhears the shooter whisper his name into an ear bud. He learns he's being hunted.

By having my idea, my protagonist, and a gripping inciting incident, all I have to do now is sit and write. The story will have Pro trying to evade capture while solving the mystery of why he is being targeted and also falling in love with Crush through various plot points.

A plot point is simply a point in the series of events that is your story. I like to think about a few major plot points before I write. One plot point is Pro and Crush entering into a relationship. Another is Pro learning he is being hunted. Another is Pro learning who is hunting him. And the main plot point, the climax of the story, will occur when Pro confronts the person targeting him. Writing becomes pretty easy for me when I know where I want the story to generally go, I just need to get the characters moving along in the direction and I can refine the plot points based on how they get there.

Of course, the plot will be influenced by the antagonist. In a good novel, the antagonist will be relatable, even if hateable. In the movie X-Men, the inciting incident is a boy being separated from his parents at a concentration camp where his powers develop as he starts bending a metal fence. Magneto develops into an understandable villain, his goal is to ensure he's not registered as a mutant and rounded up to be killed — so he has a reasonable hatred of humans.

If we want to write a good novel, our antagonist cannot merely be a thrower of obstacles, but a person with motivation for doing what they are doing. If you are having a hard time understanding why your villain is doing something, spend some time and get to know your villain. When in doubt, self-preservation is a great motivator.

Let's make our antagonist the White House Chief of Staff who uses a former secret service agent as his hitman to do his dirty work. He believes people who challenge his President will make it harder for the President to accomplish his goal of universal health care. Thus, the means of killing a few freethinkers is justified by the ends of the lives saved. This of course can and should be tweaked, because a villain's motivation is very important.

If the reader walks away thinking, *But why even bother, Pro just wanted to read a book that has no bearing on the health care system*, then we have a problem with our novel. This is part of why work-shopping your writing with others is so important. Maybe someone suggests there's a hidden code in the book that contains the location of the nuclear missiles of the United States that Pro figured it out. That's why the hitman targeted him. We can easily tweak plot points to make it a better story when we understand the antagonist's motivation.

Our plot is a series of events, right? It is much easier to adjust early plot points because each future plot point is influenced by what we've already written. This is why it is important to pause, reflect, edit, and workshop your writing as you go. When you have your work reviewed and talk about it, you learn a lot about your story and can sharpen plot points so your entire story is more compelling.

If you workshop and sharpen a really good part of your story, you can lock that plot point in and build the rest of the story around it even if it is a point in the middle of the novel. If you don't find a base to build from, you may find it overwhelming to take all your ideas and merge them into a great and cohesive plot. But if you can lock in some inciting incidents, great passages of tension and resolution, you'll find writing a novel with a good plot is quite manageable.

Some well-known writers lock-in the beginning of their novel and how it will end. They fill in the middle as they go, letting the characters take them on a journey. Others start the middle and have the characters fight their way out. Any way is fine. Just identify some major plot points to make sure your story sticks to its own path.

Before finalizing the major points, peak a few steps ahead in the process. Just like when walking, it's best to look ahead before taking your next step.

3. Find Your Target Audience

Yes. That's right. You have only an idea and rough plot for your book but you should already be thinking about your target audience. If you say "everyone" then understand that probably means "no one."

If your story involves teenage vampires, odds are that you're in the YA (young adult) category. If your story involves robot love, odds are that you're in science fiction. Of course your genre can spill over, while *Harry Potter* was written for kids, many adults enjoyed it too. But it started out and stayed consistent as a children's/young adult book – no graphic violence or sex.

Once you have an idea for your story, go to your local bookstore, library, or look online at the various categories and subcategories for what genre your book will eventually belong in. Your genre can change as your story progresses and you can cross multiple genres. But while writing your novel, keep in mind who your target audience is and how to write the best story to reach them.

Our plot involving Pro trying to figure out why he is being targeted for murder fits perfectly with the thriller genre. So read a book by Vince Flynn, Michael Connelly, or another best-selling author to see what succeeds in the genre. Understand that the thriller genre needs to have action against a ticking clock. If the story lulls too much, the core market will lose interest.

If we like the idea of making the book mostly a love story, we know we are appealing to a different market and want the plot development and character interactions in the story to reference it. When someone asks, "What's your book about?" You should be able to tell them not only what it's about in one paragraph, but also what major author it's like. Our story about Pro will be a thriller, we'll try to write it as a mystery with lots of tension, so we can say – kind of like Dan Brown or Michael Connelly if they wrote a high school student caught in a government conspiracy.

Your target market may not know if they enjoy a certain sub genre of fantasy, but they know if they like George R.R. Martin or J.R.R. Tolkien. As you write your novel, keep in mind how you will sell it so that you stay focused on writing a story that has a better chance to sell.

If your novel meanders around and you create something that's hard to describe what it's about and what it's like, it probably won't sell well. Keep your writing focused towards your target audience. Envision what shelf your book will be on at Barnes & Noble and what best-selling authors you are ranked ahead of on your genre list(s). Keeping your target audience in mind will help you write a better novel.

4. Develop Your Logline

This is not an easy task to do but it's incredibly important. If you cannot succinctly tell people what your book is about, it will be all but impossible to get them to spend their money and time reading your book.

A good logline will succinctly tell a reader a bit about the book to let them know if it's the kind of story they might be interested in. You want the logline of your book to have broad appeal, but also to be narrow enough to be honest with the reader who won't like it.

My first novel, *Wounded by Her Guardian*, is a story where, "An attorney organization's secretive inner circle starts an everyday lawyer on a path to unravel a conspiracy involving the United States Dollar."

My second novel, *Sunshine or Lead*, is a story where, "A Chinese-American kept a long-standing secret—she was sent to the United States as a child to be a spy. When her handlers try to activate her, she seeks the support of an attorney to help keep her alive and out of prison."

My third novel, *The Dinosaur Lawyer*, is a story where, "An attorney is hired to by a billionaire client to prove dinosaurs are a hoax. Initially drawn to the case only for the money, the attorney starts gathering proof and starts to believe the unthinkable—dinosaurs never existed."

My fourth novel, *Blanket Immunity*, is a story where, "A successful prosecutor loses her race for judge and starts her own law practice. Her first clients are an accused rapist, drug dealer, and murderer that bring her to a cross-roads where she has to decide if she'll work for or against a client."

These are my loglines. I'm not saying they're great, just that they are mine and should give you a sense of what each novel is about. Don't like conspiracies, you won't like my novels. Don't like lawyers, you won't like my novels. But if you like the idea of a story that follows my loglines, if my stories follow them, which they do, there is a good chance you'll enjoy my books.

With our story about Pro and Crush – how would you write a logline to sell that book? Think about it for a few minutes. Pretend you wrote the story of Pro and Crush. If you're at a book signing with your novel and someone asks, "What's it about?" How do you respond? You flip to the back cover and say some iteration of what you have on it. Write your own, it's not easy. I've got two samples for our story:

> a.   In trying to win the affection of his popular classmate, a shy student buys a book that marks him for murder by a government trying to exterminate free thinkers. Can he survive long enough to solve who's after him and win her affection?

> b.   Embarrassed by the rejection of the one girl who told him no, ultra-popular student tries to win her heart by writing a romance novel. His writing marks him by the government and the student has to risk his future as a doctor to stand up for the freedom to write and his chance at love.

We have the same idea but the logline will help us mold the plot of where we are going with story. Story A will focus us towards a thriller. So forty pages of why Crush is so worthy of Pro's affection are misplaced because we need suspense. But story B would be geared towards a different market, more emphasis on the relationship than the threat of death. The stakes in B are about his future as a doctor, not his very survival. Our plots change based upon the genre we are writing in and our novel must follow our logline.

You don't have to have your final logline down when you start writing your novel – but you want to have a rough logline written down that your novel will follow. If your novel changes course, that's fine, update your logline.

If you're writing a book and the logline is about android lovers meeting up before the government finds them to separate them, you probably don't want to have a ten-chapter criminal trial in it. You don't want to get mired down in legal procedures and stray too far from your logline because most sci-fi and romance readers are not the same people drawn to a technical courtroom drama. This is why it's important to think of our target audience and overall focus of our novel early in the process.

Basically, don't lose focus of what your book is about as you write it. Write a logline, the short description of your novel, and stick to it. If your novel veers, change your logline, or bring your novel back to your logline.

5. Create Your Storyboard/Outline

Before you write your novel, you should have a sense of who you want to read it and what it's basically about – and what's going to happen. Some people outline their entire novel before they start writing, that can be quite helpful.

While you don't have to outline before you start, once your first chapter is done, you must start an outline. Keep track of key facts, dates, times, and events on a separate document. I've done this on a legal pad and a separate Word file. I prefer the Word file. In your outline, you'll want the dates of events in your novel written down along with key facts that will need to be important later in the story.

If it takes two years, or even just six months, to write your novel – it will be hard to remember exactly what happened when as the story grows. If you're in a groove writing a scene and have to stop to remember when Pro boarded the flight to Washington D.C., it can pull you out of the groove. But being pulled out of the groove is better than writing he flew on Wednesday, only to learn that he was in a chase scene on Thursday in Chicago and suddenly all the dates and times will have to be adjusted. Or, if you and your team happen to miss the flight in editing, the reader may stop reading your story because of logic bomb. This is a real danger, not keeping track of events and time in your story can be missed when editing.

When you re-read your story and when your editors re-read your story, if there are lots of corrections to make, a logic bomb can be left in your book and it will blow up your story for the reader. Some logic bombs can be as simple as, how did Pro get a certain key? If your outline says Pro uses key in chapter 28, skim your outline to find when he gets it. Major points should be noted.

Trying to straighten everything out during a final edit will be much more complicated if you don't have a condensed outline to refer to. If you keep things organized as you go you will have a much easier time editing.

To further ease editing, I suggest saving each chapter as a separate file as you write. This makes it much easier to send to others for review and should help with your novel structure. If you name your first chapter, "Chapter_1" it's hard to know what is in that chapter when glancing at your folder. If you name it, "1_Shooting_Ends_In_Closet" you know in Chapter 1 there's a shooting that ends in the closet.

When you have thirty chapters in your novel's folder, it is easier to find a file to work on when they are named with details. You want a process that makes it easier for you to edit and rework, saving chapter by chapter and providing a detailed file name will help you accomplish that. If you maintain one massive file, it will be harder to organize and work on your novel than if you save each chapter as its own file.

It is very easy to assemble the entire novel at a later time by cutting and pasting them all together into a single file. So keep your story separated, by chapter, as you write it.

6. Character Outline/Development

A good book, movie, or TV show will invariably have great characters. A great character is a consistent character, and as they're confronted with challenges they grow. You know James Bond is going to be cool in a crisis. If he suddenly freaked out because of a spider, the reader would feel betrayed by the character and not in a good plot twist way. Bad writing has a character go from meek to hero without any development. Great writing shows us how the meek kid becomes the hero with a series of challenges and actions so that we understand and believe how the beginning character could grow to the end character.

If your character has never shot a gun in their life, let alone a person, it's going to be hard to believe they can obtain and operate a machine gun. If you do plausibly write that, the effects of killing people, zombies, or whatever would need to have a huge impact on them. If your character is a special forces operative and you know little about how they really deal with situations, find someone in the military and talk to them about what they would feel, say, and do in a situation like the one you're writing. To write a better novel, your characters need to be more than aids to get through the plot.

How the character reacts to the plot builds rapport with the reader and pulls the reader into the story. What will Pro do if he learns Crush's dad is behind the killings? By the time of that reveal, we should have a good sense of what Pro will do because we should know him. If he has two choices – tell Crush about her dad or don't, write up the tension, suspense, and then do whatever Pro would do. Not what fits your story.

It's a great day when you want your character to get on the plane to advance the plot, but you say to yourself, "Pro would never do that." Pause. Relax. Now think of what Pro would do and find another way to get him to your plot point. It could be as simple as thugs drug him and bring him on the plane. Now you have to write his escape – but it is better to stay true to your character and figure out how you want to get to the plot point than betray your character.

Every good story is enhanced by good characters and character development. The reader roots for Harry Potter because he is constantly good. His powers develop in a reasonable manner as do his relationships with the other characters to make the reader feel invested in whatever happens to him next.

While Harry is constantly good, the viewer also roots for Tony Soprano, a murderer and serial adulterer. Tony feels depression, love, and loss. How he deals with the stress of being a mob boss makes for an excellent show and these two characters make a perfect juxtaposition. If Harry Potter cheated on Ginny Weasley, the reader would be angry with the author for the character betraying who we know Harry to be. If Tony Soprano hired a lawyer to sue his neighbor for leaves blowing on his property, we would be angry because we expect impulsive Tony to walk over with a chain saw and cut down the tree – or maybe even cut the guys legs off.

If you're ever stuck, ask yourself: what would Harry Potter do? What would Tony Soprano do? Then, what would my character do?

In *Harry Potter*, Harry is at the birthday party for Dudley and does his best to hide his jealousy and to support Dudley. If that was Tony Soprano, we would expect him to rumble down the stairs in his bathrobe, piss all over the presents, grab the cake and a bottle of booze and go outside. The different characters in your book should react differently to a circumstance – and their actions must be consistent with themselves.

Remember, Tony got the way he was because as a kid he saw his dad beat a man – and Tony didn't flinch. His growth to mob boss was easy to follow. Harry is harder to understand how he kept such a sweet nature growing up under the stairs. But Harry is consistent and never loses his sweet nature, even when on the run from Voldemort when it really hits the fan.

We really get to know Tony and Harry because they go through so much in their books and on the show. That's exactly what we want to do with our characters, show readers how the characters act, so the reader can judge for themselves if they like Harry, Tony, Pro, or Crush.

Our goal is to make Pro and Crush pop off the page just like Harry Potter and Tony Soprano. To do that, we don't tell the reader to like a character, we show them what the character does and let the reader conclude Harry is sweet and Tony is a mixed bag.

7. Show, Don't Tell

In a good novel, the author doesn't tell, the author paints a picture with words so the reader sees, smells, hears, and feels a scene and makes the conclusion about the character or event on their own.

Let's say you have a character who is financially savvy and willing to take risks. Don't tell the reader, "Fred is driven, smart, and savvy" – let the reader determine these things based on what the character does and says. Show the reader how Fred made his money. Write a passage of a past business deal where he succeeded. Or that he read about Apple developing the first iPhone and sold his blood, house, and car to buy stock options in Apple. Show us that Fred is successful and savvy, don't tell us.

Yes, I understand it's impossible to show everything – your book would be way too long and have way too many tangents if every time you wanted to introduce a character you did a flashback to an incident that shaped your character, so this is a balance you have to strike. But understand, what pulls a reader into the story is a scene we can picture. Let's compare:

A cocky, wealthy, real estate mogul asked the waiter for a glass of wine.

We can kind of picture the scene, but if this is our writing style the reader will tire because they are simply hearing the author tell them the wine orderer is cocky. Compare that with:

A balding man's solid gold cufflinks reflected a flicker of candlelight. "Chateau d'Yquem," he commanded of the waiter.

The latter is an example of showing. The reader sees a balding man and can conclude wealth and cockiness based on the expensive cufflinks and command of the waiter. The description pulls the reader into the scene, which allows your characters to comment and interact with the real estate mogul and lets the reader determine based on the moguls actions that he is cocky.

We want our readers to picture what we're writing. To best do this, we don't write conclusions, we write facts to let the reader conclude. We don't write: Pro was happy he kissed Crush. We do write: Pro smiled wide at the taste her of her mint Chapstick. We don't write: Pro is likeable. We do write: Pro helped the little old lady across the street.

This is quite hard to do well. We don't want to bore the reader by over-describing everything, a habit that I unfortunately have, but we want to put enough details so the reader can visualize our story and make conclusions about our characters on their own. If you feel you must tell the reader some information instead of showing them, make sure you do it at an opportune time and it's not simply a dump of information.

In a great story, the reader can identify what your character is experiencing because the reader feels like they are in the story. If the reader is picturing Pro walking through his high school, heart pounding, about to ask Crush out for the first time, then the author cuts in to talk about all the various trophies in the case and the school's history as he passes them, the reader is pulled out of the story and feels the author telling information. This is a no-no.

The author telling the reader the trophy information is quite like pausing the story to hand the reader a pamphlet to provide information. Do not do this. Even if the information is interesting and important, do not pull the reader out of the story to give them information.

When Harry Potter goes to the sorting hat, we don't know everything there is to know about the four school houses, we know his friends have been put into one house and his rival into another house. We don't need all the information right away. We know Harry wants into Gryffindor, the stakes are understood without the author telling us everything about the house right then and there. Keep your reader in the moment, don't slip them a pamphlet about the history of Gryffindor just as Harry is walking up to the sorting hat.

The key to engrossing writing that sucks the reader in, so they can't close the book, is to keep them visualizing your story. We do this by writing enough description to show the reader what we want them to conclude, not tell them.

In my writing group, the following passage was submitted. First, you may note passage is writing in present tense (with tense inconsistencies). I strongly suggest you write in past tense, writing in present tense is far more difficult (if you want more information on tenses, do a Google search for Writer's Digest on tense because they have a fantastic piece on it). But this lesson is about show, don't tell. The writer submitted:

Conrad has never been chauffeured before and after his bags are put in the large Mercedes Sprinter Limo, he kisses Kate goodbye again, and again.

With a very simple change, we write:

"I've never been chauffeured before." A big grin spread across Conrad's face. While the driver put his bags in the black Mercedes limo, he kissed Kate goodbye again, and again.

This is a subtle change, the first version has the author telling you that Conrad has never been in a limo before. The second version, Conrad, not the author tells that information. It's Conrad's voice, not the author's voice. Plus Conrad reacts to the information so we picture him smiling. Plus we described the limo as black – a little description that makes the scene easier to visualize. And the passage is a bit easier to read because we switched to past tense.

Showing and not telling is a difficult. Sometimes it's just so much more efficient to write: Pro was excited to see Crush, rather than: Pro's heart pounded, his palms grew clammy, his eyes widened, and his smile grew when Crush turned the corner. If we write every single detail, all the time, the reader may lose interest in the story because stuff needs to happen.

So you have to strike a balance – understand that your goal is to engross the reader by showing them most of the information in your novel, not telling them. But you also can't describe every single emotion at all times. The goal is to make sure the reader is pulled into the story and the best way to do that is consistently show what you want them to picture, not tell them what you want them to know. This is an area of feedback you will get when you workshop your writing, are you overshowing so the pacing gets too slow or are you telling too much so it's hard to get sucked into the story.

If there is vital plot or background information that you just need to tell the reader, a great way to communicate that information is through dialogue. Dialogue can help you "tell" information and keep the story moving at your ideal pace.

8. Use Dialogue Effectively

Some novels have tremendous amounts of dialogue, others, little to none. I tend to like a good amount of dialogue because it's a perfect way for readers to hear my characters' voices and attitudes.

First tip, the word 'said' can stick out like a sore thumb if repeated in dialogue.

Pro said, "Hi."

"Hi," Crush said.

"I stubbed my toe earlier," Pro said.

"Oh no," Crush said.

While the dialogue itself is unremarkable, the 'saids' are tiresome. Replacing the one dialogue tag with a synonym is a partial cure (switch said to whispered, gasped, stated, etc.). Instead, leave out most of the 'saids' and add some actions.

"Hi, Crush," Pro said with a sheepish grin.

"Hi."

"I stubbed my toe earlier." Pro grimaced as he watched her move a strand of hair away from her face, looking for signs of sympathy.

"Oh no!" Crush pointed at the bus barreling towards them.

The great thing about writing – you can always write in a bus about to run someone over to spice up the scene. Now if the point of this passage is Pro trying to woo Crush, a little bit of unremarkable dialogue is okay if the reader is put into the head of one of the two. There should be a purpose to the conversation.

Dialogue can be very effective in getting to know characters, especially if the reactions are described, and this can also be a great way of getting out information to advance the plot. So long as it is done in a believable way.

Do not have your characters regurgitate information to help the reader understand your plot. Your dialogue will make your characters flat if they are just a means to dump information:

> "My dad is the Chief of Staff for the President. He went to college at Harvard, then went to business school at Wharton. When he finished, he started working at Sears where he got his first big break. Now he's trying to save Sears from going out of business as part of the President's task force." Crush said with enthusiasm.

> Pro looked at her with confusion. "No duh, I've been his intern for six months and know all of this."

Your story will bore readers and you will lose author credibility if characters are just regurgitating background information. If you need to info dump, parse it out. Let only the important information come out of your characters as they flirt or fight through dialog or action:

> "I'm sorry I didn't go to Harvard like your father!" Pro yelled, slamming the cabinet door.

> Crush's eyes glistened as tears formed. "I—I—I just thought this could be your big break like he had at Sears."

I'm not sure why Sears and Harvard are plot points in the story, but if they exchange a bit of information in a fight, you can show how they fight, how they make up, and build the tension and drama. It will also build intrigue for what happened with Sears, so a flashback or telling the story to a reflection (character used so that your other character can state information) would be a way to bring that necessary information to the reader. This could be accomplished by Pro talking with his friend after the fight, the friend asks, what was her dad's big break at Sears? Then Pro can talk about it and give that information to the reader naturally.

This should remind you of the show, don't tell, pamphlet problem. You want to communicate Crush's Dad's resume to the reader, but the problem is, reading a resume isn't exciting. But how a great secondary character, a reflection, supports or makes fun of Pro can be exciting or interesting.

Or we can have Pro and Crush be interviewed by a reporter, while Crush is answering questions about her dad, the reader gets inside Pro's head. Maybe Pro can't stop fantasizing about Crush, maybe he makes snarky internal comments that add humor to the scene. Maybe you separate Pro and Crush and each talk to their best friend.

Sometimes a baseball manager taps his left arm to signal bringing in the left-handed pitcher from the bullpen when they need help getting an important out. If you need to get important information to the reader, bring in the leftie. Bring in a reflection, a secondary character that can listen to the information you want to dump – but bring us into the scene and make the characters pop off the page with interesting interactions and reactions. Slam doors. Yell. Scream. Cry. Gather supplies to bury the body.

We use reflections because your story will lose credibility if your characters say things they both know:

"Remember how we searched in the abandoned warehouse and found this key, right before Dave died." Pro said as he pulled a key from his pocket.

"Yes. I can't believe your best friend died from a gunshot wound."

Instead, try to weave the information into your story and intriguing dialogue:

"Dave," Pro said sullenly as he clenched a key in his fist.

Crush gently placed her hands on his fist. "He would want us to finish what we started in that warehouse."

My friend, author David Larson, refers to the clenched fist and character movements as body language attributions ("BLAs"). If you have a page of dialogue, you should have BLAs breaking it up. A character pauses to stir a drink, takes a sip, smiles, frowns, nods a head, etc. Remember that characters and the story don't completely stop for dialogue, even sitting at a dinner table, there are scents, tastes, and sounds to describe. A BLA can also identify who is speaking:

"Ann!" Sara called out from across the room.

"Hi."

The reader can infer the next person speaking is Ann. When possible, try not to have the word 'said' appear on a page more than three or four times.

Good dialogue includes actions, reactions, and somewhat believable conversation. This is your novel, not real life, so you can write a bit more information in your dialogue than would normally occur, but can't go too far.

Capture your character's voices and let them speak to write a better novel. And if Pro and Crush wouldn't have a particular conversation, bring in a reflection. Let Crush talk to her mom, or Pro talk to his buddy. Have your dialogue stay believable by bringing in a different person if you want to tell more information than two characters normally would.

9. Find Your Characters' Voices

Not every character should sound exactly the same. Some should speak in shorter sentences. Some should use poor grammar. Some should be very formal, some informal. It all depends on the character. Once you determine how your character speaks, stay consistent.

A friend of mine, Brian Hogan, is writing a fantastic science fiction novel about an android, from the point of view of the android. In the first drafts, sometimes the android would sound like a human, other times in exacting computer-speak. In one early chapter he described blades of grass using metric measurements, pigment, and size where he got the voice just right. But then described leaves on trees with an adjective like beautiful. It didn't seem to jive within the same chapter. Brian did some re-work and he found his character's voice that made the story even more enjoyable because it felt like we really got to know the android as it became more consistent. It was a small but important change, one that came about because of his membership in a writing group and a great example for us to find out characters' voices.

If we have Pro talking like a "bro" throughout the book, it wouldn't make sense for him to deliver a formal plea to the Chief of Staff in the end. We would expect him to say, "Come on bro," or things of that nature. Now if you want him to talk like a bro sometimes, but be able to wax poetic others, that's fine, if it's set up. Maybe at the initial school shooting he receives an A on an English paper and speaks clearly to his grandmother when asking to borrow her car, so that when the big speech comes the reader still believes it is the Pro they got to know and not the author being lazy and changing the character to fit the story.

While I suggest the use of slang and short sentences, you don't want to make characters hard to understand. You don't want to go overboard and make a character mispronounce too many words or speak in too strange of an accent, nothing that makes your story hard to follow. If it's hard to make the actual language different, you can have characters interact differently with objects. Maybe one smiles at puppies, another tries to kick them. One starts speaking with short sentences but they get longer as the conversation progresses. Your characters' dialogue and internal thoughts should feel different from each other.

As a thought exercise, let's say that Pro loses in a game of chess to Crush. If we swap Pro for Harry Potter he would say:

"Great match, Crush." Harry sighed as he reached his hand to shake hers. *I can learn from this. Rooks are very valuable pieces.*

But if Tony Soprano loses he would say:

"Ah, dumb game." Tony waived his meaty arm across the board, knocking over all the pieces. He glared, *I want smash your face in.*

Pro would say:

"I didn't see that rook coming. Brains and beauty! Bam!" Pro winked, then gave her a big smile.

To have great characters, you need to be consistent with their voice in dialogue, inner thoughts, and actions. This doesn't mean using stereotyped accents or actions. It means giving your character individuality. We are writing Pro as kind of a bro, kind of sweet, and crushing heavily on Crush. So we communicate that in dialogue or his inner thoughts and stick to it.

For other characters, maybe one uses car metaphors a lot. Another always proselytizes about being vegan. It doesn't matter, what matters is making your characters deep and multi-layered, just like real people you know. And let that come out consistently. If a character has real traits, they will jump off the page. Your reader will root for your hero to succeed and your villain to fail.

The reader won't invest in the story as much if the secondary characters are flat. If Crush is just a pretty face who sits there, readers aren't going to root for Pro to be with her.

If you write characters way over the top, they will be caricatures and you'll have the same problem.

If you write relatable characters that are consistent with their own unique voice, you will write a better novel.

10. Do Not Shift Points of View Willy-Nilly

Writing a book in 1st person means the story is told from the point of view of the character. If we are writing our story with Pro in the first person, our story would read:

I walked into class. When I saw her, I held my breath. It took all my concentration to sit down without falling over.

In 3rd person, it means someone else is telling the story, we can jump into a character's head, but we don't live there.

He stopped breathing when he saw her. It took every ounce of focus to sit down without falling over. *Should I smile at her?*

FYI - The italics are Pro's actual thoughts. It's written like internal dialogue and can be very effective at putting the reader inside your character's head.

Regardless of which method you choose to write in, you don't want to jump around and switch from point of view ("POV") to another character's point of view. I write in the 3rd person omniscient so I had a hard time under-standing why people in my writing group were complaining about point of view shifts.

I'm ashamed to admit, it wasn't until writing my fourth novel that I really understood the problem with zooming in on one character and then another. It's really simple, "head hopping" causes confusion for the reader. The jumping around from one POV to another POV makes the story harder to follow, unless it is done really well. It truly hit home for me when I listened to the audiobook of my third novel where I had to say, wait, who's thinking that – and I was the one who wrote it. I felt like an idiot for not understanding this years ago and hope I'm communicating this clearly to you so you have a head start on me when I wrote my first three novels. To make it clear, let's go through an example and write Pro and Crush at lunch:

I can't believe how hot she is. Pro's face flushed red while he tried to think of something to say. "Uh, what's good here?" he asked.

"I like the chopped salad," she said with a little smile. She couldn't believe Pro finally asked her out. "Are you feeling okay?"

"Yeah, why?" He reached for his water glass, feeling his face redden further with embarrassment.

She shrugged, thankful the waiter approached and was excited to order. She skipped breakfast and was afraid her stomach might start making funny noises.

"You guys ready?" The waiters eyes widened with recognition, embarrassed to serve the seniors at the school he just graduated from and not be off at college.

Pro set his glass down.

She couldn't believe how handsome he was.

With the above passage we're bouncing from one POV to another. With just two people and such mundane information it's not terribly hard to follow. But once the waiter comes in, the story becomes harder to know whose thinking what. As written, the reader wonders if Crush thinks Pro or the waiter is handsome. It's hard to tell because we are hopping from head to head and aren't getting consistency. As authors, we do not want to confuse readers, we want to make it easy for them to understand the story we're telling.

If you want to shift POV, ideally it should be signaled at each chapter or scene break. Shifting POV's within a chapter should be rare, try to stick to one POV per scene. If you do shift POV's, make it clear and natural that you are shifting the POV. Let's say we are in Pro's POV and want to switch to Crush:

Enough sipping, time to say something clever. Pro set his glass of iced tea down.

"Can I have a sip?" Crush asked, looking at the glass.

"Sure."

Crush took the glass and smiled. She felt the cool condensation against her skin and refreshed after taking two large gulps of tea. "Thank you."

"You're welcome."

She blushed. "Oh no, I got gloss on your glass."

We used the glass to transfer the POV. While it still might be jarring to hop from head to head, it's a little less so because of the glass transition. In short passages like the above, with only two people, the POV shifts aren't jarring, but in a longer passage, if we are in Crush's head thinking about her choice of shoes, the reader may say – wait, was this Pro or Crush for the last five pages thinking about football?

I would have sold more copies of my books had I stuck to POV's and focused on smooth transitions of POV because my stories would have been easier to read. The last thing you want is a reader to stop and say, wait, what? Then go back, re-read, or even worse, close the book.

11. Chapter Length and Structure

The average chapter should be about 2,500 words. Of course, a 5,000-word chapter or 500-word chapter can work perfectly well. Feel free to use small chapters, even one page, if you've got several character arcs and story lines – but generally try to stay in the 2000-3000 word range.

Chapter length is important to your potential readers. Grab three books that you loved and read the first three chapters to see how they did it. Great chapters are not arbitrary break points. The next chapter in our life is common parlance for doing something different in the next stage of our life – because chapters are different.

Generally chapters are used to give the reader a break or to allow the writer to shift. A 15,000-word chapter will make the reader feel like they're trapped in the story. A series of 500-word chapters might make the reader feel like they are bouncing around too much.

If we are writing Pro asking Crush out on a date and the scene is at a natural end with the chapter at only 800 words, we can skip to their date in the same chapter with a scene break. Place three or four stars or dots in the center of the page. This signifies we are shifting to a different time or place, but still within the same chapter.

* * *

A scene break isn't a new chapter. A scene break is like a commercial break in the middle of a television episode. If your book is like a television series, think of chapters like episodes. Ideally most chapters will have a mini plot that will be resolved, with the occasional cliffhanger. Use the inherent structure of chapters to your advantage. How do you feel when you finish a chapter? If a book is reading smoothly for me, I love the way they stack up. I may look at the clock and note, I have thirty minutes left, I can get three more chapters in. As a reader, I set a goal to read three more chapters before I close the book.

Your goal is to write a story where the reader keeps turning pages and asks the three words that matter most: what happens next?

The best way to do that is write compelling paragraph after compelling paragraph and engaging chapter after engaging chapter. When you stack several great chapters together, you'll have a great novel.

In the beginning of our story, we have Pro at high school, the shooting chapter. If the chapter gets to 4,000 words because so much happened, I would split it into two chapters, maybe the first ends when they reach the closet. Nice and short, close the chapter on an interesting note and make the reader want to turn the page and find out what happens in the next chapter.

The aftermath of the shooting will be a new chapter. Discovering the relationship between the book and the murders, another chapter. Different things should happen in different chapters. So much so, that if you want to go back to re-read about Pro's time in high school, you should be able to identify a chapter or two for the reader to go back to. If there are a dozen flashbacks within each chapter, the book will be harder to read. Use chapters as an aid to make the structure of your book tell a story that is easier to read.

And I suggest your first chapter be on the shorter side, 2,000 words max – preferably 1,500 – with a compelling hook.

Consider how you shop for a book. If you're like me, you look at the cover and title, if intrigued, you flip to the back and read the logline. This is what almost every reader does. If they're on the fence after reading the back cover, they open to the first chapter and start reading. If you can get them to read a well-written first chapter so they want to know what happens next, they are likely to buy your book and read chapter after chapter until they finish. That's the goal.

If you make your goal to write great chapter, after great chapter, they will stack up, and that's when you'll have a great novel.

12. Novel Length

Depending on your genre, different word counts tend to be proper. For young adult, you are probably looking around 50-80,000. For a thriller or drama, 70-90,000. For science fiction, 100-120,000. These are general guidelines, not rules. If you need to build a world, like you do in fantasy or science fiction, your book will need to be longer. If you are writing for a younger audience, your books should be simpler, thus they will tend to be a little shorter.

In reality, your book should be the absolute minimum number of words necessary to develop your plot and characters. You may find you have written an amazing passage, even an entire chapter, but find it doesn't help advance your plot or character development. Chances are, it should be removed from your novel – and saved to hopefully be placed in a future work.

Do you know a person that tells ten tangential stories before finishing the tale they're telling you? You ask how the car accident happened, he says, "And an orange flew into the windshield. I got the orange at Trader Joe's. I was at the grocery before the accident. And I couldn't even find parking there, so had to walk like two full blocks. And I forgot to bring my bags with, so I had to put the orange in my pocket and my hands were full." Don't tell your story like that guy.

The orange origin story does not add to the overall story or character development of your novel – so skip it. Or if you really want to tell it, since this is fiction, there better be a chase scene through the Trader Joe's parking lot so the tangent is actually a setup for something that will happen later. But when you find something you've written doesn't help advance the plot or character development – it probably doesn't belong, even if it's some of your best writing.

In my first novel, I had a scene in my head that would be the end of the book. It involved the lead character at a remote cabin taking on corrupt secret service agents. When I finished that, I was at 50,000 words. There wasn't enough story in my story. Luckily, so much was built up to that point that it was very easy to keep the story going. I was able to have a new inciting incident regarding the fallout from that scene and how it affected the hero and the country. The novel grew to 90,000 words. In hindsight, it would have been better if I cut about 10,000 words, about 3-4 chapters from the beginning, because the book started out a bit slow. It finished fast and well – but a slow start doesn't bode well for sales.

The length of your novel is very important to hit your pacing. A story shouldn't feel like it's dragging on, but it also has to be substantial enough to warrant spending money on the book.

To keep pacing, many writers split their novel up into Acts. At the end of a short Act 1 is the inciting incident which launches your hero into action. Act 2 your hero running into conflict after conflict trying to solve the problem. Act 3 is the climax and resolution.

You can identify the structure any way you like. Call it a beginning, middle, and end, Act 1, 2, and 3. It doesn't matter. The key is having something kick off the story, the story, a reveal, and tying up loose ends. You want enough words to flesh out your characters so they don't feel flat. You want enough words so you can incite, build tension, have a climax, and resolve your plot and subplots.

When setting your approximate word goal, keep in mind that it's a lot easier for a reader to finish a shorter story than a long story. It is also easer for a reader to start a shorte tory than a longer story. How many times have you stare thousand-page classic and said, "Maybe next time," picked up a shorter book?

I've found by writing in my genre, about 3C 2,500 words puts the novel at 75,000 words. T perfect for telling a story with a compelling plot, fully developed characters, and a resolution.

I use words as the length because font size, spacing, etc. can make page count more difficult to compare. This book is about 19,000 words, about one quarter of a novel.

Overall novel length and chapter length are very important. Generally speaking, shorter is better because it's more manageable. If you send someone 3000 words or less to review your first chapter, you'll probably get their help. If you send someone 19,000 words to edit – you probably won't.

13. Determine Your Ending

How is your story resolved? Does Pro end up happily married to Crush after killing her father? Is there a huge shock and Pro is killed by Crush who supports her father's dream of exterminating free thinkers? If you have a love interest between Pro and Crush, along with the running for his life, you want to resolve both major issues near the end of your book.

If you have six smaller issues, like Pro making things right with Dave's family for his death, or Crush's mom turning on her dad, you don't want to forget about them if you've set them up.

If your book is part of a series, then you may not have to resolve everything, but you do want to address your major plot points. Provide at least partial resolution, maybe even an inciting incident. Make sure plot points and sub-plot points are addressed and are at a good spot to leave off – just like when you close out a chapter.

You have spent a lot of time getting to your ending. It is the last thing the reader will read before they determine if they are going to recommend your book to others or write a book review. The beginning and end of your book are incredibly important, so take your time with them.

If you're like me, you probably tire of the project near the end, especially with the end so close. But make sure you spend a lot of time on the ending, resolve as much as possible, and give a big payout to the reader who spent all the time reading the entire story.

A good beginning will help with your first sale, a good ending will help with referrals for a lot more sales.

14. Climaxes are Important

If you are resolved that Pro will best Crush's dad and win Crush's heart, then you should put obstacle after obstacle in Pro's way that will be resolved in an exciting moment. The suspense, the angst, the intrigue, should all build until the reader can't wait to see what happens. Then we have Crush moving a gun back and forth between her dad and Pro – before finally pulling the trigger.

The more we care for the characters, the more the story builds tension, the more powerful the climax will become and more memorable the story will be.

In the opening chapter we have the school shooting, the tension builds as Pro and Crush hide in the closet. They make a break for it and bump into Dave. The three escape the school and make it a few blocks to a warehouse and when the shooter catches up to Pro and Crush, Dave jumps off a huge crate and knocks him over. While trying to subdue him, a key falls out of the shooter's pocket that Crush grabs. Pro runs to help Dave when the shooter kills Dave with his last bullet. He aims at Pro but the gun clicks empty, and while the shooter changes the clip Pro and Crush escape, leaving Dave behind.

At Dave's funeral his little brother Jimmy is crying, lamenting that Dave won't make it to his big brother event, to make Pro more likeable, we have him offer to go in Dave's place. Then maybe he misses it because of the main plot, and he needs to make amends to Dave's parents and Jimmy. Or maybe at the end he gets on Air Force One and the President and Pro appear at the event with Jimmy. A good story will need to have secondary characters and secondary plots that weave together and need resolution. If it turns out the big brother event isn't needed in the ending, it should be cut from the story in its entirety.

If you can naturally resolve more than one plot point at the same time with the ultimate climax, that's fantastic. If we have Crush set up to choose between Pro and her dad as one plot point, and if Pro will best her dad as another, when we have Crush resolve both of those at the same time — we have higher stakes in the outcome. That's the goal, raise the stakes with each chapter until everything comes to a head.

If our story was the focus of the love story and not the thriller, we can still have high stakes. Crush decides if she will follow her father's wishes and go to an all women's college in Oklahoma or if she will choose to be with Pro. At the same time she's making her decision, a woman, Second Choice, who has a crush on Pro is professing her love to him. He realizes he has feelings for Second Choice too. You can write the story to have emotional peaks. While choosing who to kill is different than who to love, the emotional stakes are quite similar. You write the story to build tension, and build more tension, until the climax — then make it a compelling decision or happening that stays true to your characters.

Have several climaxes in your story and one big one near the end to write a better novel.

15. Inciting Incidents

Your novel is a path that peaks at the climax and ends with a resolution. It will also need an inciting incident. Not only do you need forks in the road and reasons for the story to move forward, but you to have a compelling reason why. The more compelling the inciting incident, the more compelling the story.

Our story starts with Pro reading this book before class starts and the school shooter enters. He overhears the shooter searching for him. That's an inciting incident for the first act of the major plot: will Pro find a way to survive? This naturally sets us up to resolve the first issue, why is he being targeted, which leads to a climax and then another inciting incident, discovering there is a program. That leads to another climax and resolution that Crush's dad is behind the program. Which leads to another climax and resolution that Crush will have to choose between Pro and her dad.

A great story will have several inciting incidents each with its own mini climax and resolution, which then incites the next part of the story. While you want your story to build and build, your reader should naturally get steps tied up and behind them, which brings them to the next part of your story. You need to have new inciting incidents within your book to ensure you have good pacing.

A gripping inciting incident doesn't have to be life or death, but it should feel that way. A character clearing their throat, looking out at a packed audience and fighting through stage fright is a compelling opening – we just have to make sure the inciting incident fits with whatever the plot is.

16. Find Your Story Pace

All stories have peaks and valleys. A 200-page c
is too much and will become boring. A 20-page intros
on if Crush could like Pro is going to be boring for a thr
Good writing builds tension, then breaks it. Then builds ag
then breaks again. Valleys in the action give readers a chance
to catch their breath as you build towards it again.

Your chapters can be all peak, all valley, and some of each.
But your entire story requires some levels of peak excitement,
and some time to relax and let the story build. Keep in mind
there are different kind of peaks, while Pro joining Crush and
her dad for dinner isn't a peak like a chase scene, it can be an
emotional peak if we know that her dad wants Pro dead and
Pro is trying to stop her dad. That should be a very tense
dinner – and maybe the inciting incident for who Crush will
choose to support.

Small details can pay huge dividends. Let's say Pro and
Crush are hitting it off and she invites him to her cousin's
wedding in three weeks. Let's say we've revealed to the reader
that Crush's dad is the bad guy, the reader will see tension
coming when Pro and Crush's dad meet at the wedding. So
now the time spent at the tux rental place is suddenly tense,
will Crush's dad see him there? Maybe it's a near miss,
building further tension. If we put a small detail into the story,
it can help our natural valleys build more tension for the
payout.

Use natural lulls in action to help the reader get to know
your character and to set things up that will be coming later.
But always keep your story going. Do this by having inciting
incidents, climaxes, and resolutions throughout your novel.
Do not let several chapters go by without having something
important triggered or something important resolved.

ʼry

veloped your characters, gave
ed out how to resolve them, and
vith peaks and valleys. In each
·et, this is your story and any
k or every other source should
t to accomplish.

...uing novels has been a fantastic experience for me. It helped me meet new friends, become a better legal writer, given me great small talk at parties and events, has given me a sense of accomplishment, and has made a tiny bit of money. While all my novels could be greatly improved with the techniques I've learned and outlined here, I'm still proud of the stories and what people get from them. My goal was to tell stories to entertain people and get them to think about issues like monetary policy, immigration, and challenging firmly held beliefs (dinosaurs being a hoax). By my definition, I am a successful novelist. I had stories in me, got to tell them the way I wanted, and I can stand behind them as pretty good stories.

If your purpose is to make money selling novels, honestly, you are probably better off doing something else to make money. The starving artist cliché is cliché for a reason. Most authors won't make much money selling their novels. Consider J.K. Rowling had publishers pass on *Harry Potter* 12 times before it was picked up. Her series went on to sell over 450 million copies worldwide.

Your book could be one of the best and most profitable books ever written, yet you may still go undiscovered. If you tell the story you want to tell, if you write at a level that others enjoy reading, your writing can be a success even if you don't sell millions of copies.

The key is to write a book you are proud of. That you can honestly recommend to your friends and strangers. If you find you're getting negative feedback, you have more work to do before you can publish with pride. And that's okay. When a friend doesn't love it, we listen and try to make some changes. Writing a novel is a process. Re-work your novel until you're happy with it and so are people who read it. That's when it's ready to sell.

You've told your story. You've edited it. You've work shopped it with other writers. You've had a friend read it. Another friend read it. You're almost done.

Unless you have a great team, and even with a great team, you should probably pay for a professional editor. This will help catch poor grammar, typos, and identify plot bombs or character flaws. Depending on the length of the novel, a professional editor could cost a thousand dollars or more. If you've disagreed with your friend's suggestions, chances are you will be more willing to listen to someone you pay to find flaws. And remember, finding flaws helps you create a better final copy if you fix them.

I did not pay for a professional editor with my first four novels. I relied on my wife and a few friends. Eventually I found that my friend Dennis Quinn, an avid reader, is a fantastic plot editor. My aunt Mary Van Susteren is a fantastic grammar and character development editor. My brother Joe is quite good at both language and story. My wife is a fantastic proof reader, but was hesitant to criticize my writing. It took trial and error to find out what balance worked for me.

I now have my writing group that I work with as I go, my team of four volunteers plus Pete Smegielski as a finish reader, and I can tell that my novels are much more polished. I probably need to bite the bullet and invest in a professional editor to really take the next step – but I invite you to take an hour and go read the first few chapters of my novels that Amazon previews for free. Check out the difference in my writing as I learned and what my team, and my writing group, have helped me accomplish.

As I've stated often, you need to have other people help with your book. If you want to find a professional editor, start by asking other writers you know for a referral. If you don't know any other writers yet, go back and review the path of writing a novel – you cannot finish a novel without other people reading it first. If your writing friends don't have a professional editor they can recommend, you can find an editor at Upwork.com, Craigslist, or with a Google search. I suggest checking to see if you can get them to edit your first three chapters for a set price. That will get you a sense of what they can do for you and how receptive you will be to their editing process before you commit a lot of money. Spending money to edit the entire project without knowing the benefit is a big risk that you can mitigate by having a portion of the book edited at a time.

Once you've got your fully edited, as perfect as possible manuscript, it's time to submit it to an agent or to self-publish.

18. Submitting Your Manuscript to an Agent

Your story is complete. For format, generally agents want one inch margins all around, spacing at double, and font at size twelve for Times New Roman. With that you have your finished manuscript but want to check the requirements of any agent you submit to.

If you want a chance at a big publisher accepting your book, you need a literary agent to take your book there. Use www.QueryTracker.com or *Writer's Market* yearly publication to find agents and publishers who specialize in your genre. Be prepared to spend a lot of time trying to find agents to send queries to and work on your query letter for each agent. This is almost exactly like submitting a resume and cover letter.

Once you identify an agent seeking submissions in your genre, submit to them online as they request. Often they want the first chapter or first ten pages, along with background information of the author and a synopsis of your story. This is where your well defined logline will really pay dividends as will your social media presence you've been cultivating.

You can attend writer's conferences and look for in person ways to talk with literary agents. Either way takes time.

I met two literary agents at a writing convention in San Diego. One was interested, I ended up meeting with that agent two years later and handed him a manuscript for my fourth book. I waited for six months for him to read it but he didn't even read the first page. So I asked if he was going to read it or if I should self-publish. He suggested I self-publish.

Unfortunately, I don't have a ton of experience here to help you with landing an agent. A literary agent passed on Harry Potter. A dozen publishers passed on Harry Potter. There are so many books out there right now, so many stories, that it is really hard to break into the industry. All I can say is that if you want a traditional publisher you need to meet with agents. You need to respectfully get them to read your manuscript and hope they think they can sell it.

That process requires perseverance. If I didn't have a law practice to run I would spend a lot more time trying to get agents to read my books. I've sent about ten queries to agents I found online and received a formal rejection back from two, no word from the other eight. If you think you've got a story that will sell big, don't give up, find agents online and at conferences and find ways to give them your manuscript.

I will also urge caution when selecting an agent. Be extremely skeptical of any agent that wants you to pay them a fee. If you find a guarantee of publishing from an agent, the promise is probably too good to be true. The agent and publisher may set up the contract where they risk nothing, have no real investment, but obtain a windfall if the book catches on and sells. Based upon double hearsay, I understand some agents work with small publishers and require the author do all the marketing, then the agent and publisher take a cut of anything you sold, without providing any support.

In my opinion, there is no point in handing over a sizeable portion of your book sales if you are doing all your own marketing. Before signing any contract, considering investing in having an attorney look it over, or at the very least, read it over carefully to understand exactly what each party's rights and obligations are and ask questions in writing so they can explain what provisions mean, in writing.

You've read this book for my advice. I suggest you take a shot by reaching out to at least ten agents to see if one might be interested in your work. If you get decent feedback but no interest, reach out to another ten. Keep notes of who you submitted to and on what dates. Always be gracious in rejection because it's the right thing to do and you don't want a bad reputation for an industry you are trying to break into.

If you don't find one you think will be a good fit for you. You can self-publish. The self-publish alternative is not a bad second choice, it is relatively simple, gives you complete control, and all the profit. If you self-publish, publishers will not want to buy that book unless it's a huge success. *Fifty Shades of Grey* was self-published, then a major publisher took interest and the book was huge. That is the extreme exception.

If you choose to self-publish, your book will be one of many, but you will have a book that is available for sale on Amazon or another major website and that in of itself is really cool. Plus, you won't have to pay any percent of your revenue to an agent or receive a fraction of the publisher's profit when your book sells.

One of the coolest things for me as a writer was reading a review for my first novel, the reviewer was a person I've never met, they said they bought my book after reading *The Dinosaur Lawyer*. They enjoyed my third book so much they went and bought the first. That was a fantastic feeling and one I look to duplicate.

My friend, author Pendelton C. Wallace, has had an agent at times and self-published at others. He is quite good at marketing and has sold many thousands of copies of his novels. He makes real money self-publishing and that is the course I plan to take.

Here's the bottom line, if you can honestly stand behind your creation and respectfully ask people to give your story a read, you will be on your path towards being a profitable writer whether you find an agent or self-publish.

19. Creating Your Book

Your book needs a title. I like something unique but tried too hard with my first two book titles. *Wounded by Her Guardian* refers to the United States Dollar being wounded by politicians. But people who hear the title think it's a love story. *Sunshine or Lead* refers to exposing secrets or going to war, some people think it's a western. *The Dinosaur Lawyer* puts the existence of dinosaurs on trial. That title is my best to date.

People hear *The Dinosaur Lawyer* and understand a lawyer's involved, understand dinosaurs are involved, and are generally curious. Before you pick your title, make sure you think of several possible titles. You want something that is ear catching and also refers to your story. Give your title thought as you write and have at least two different options when you create your book cover. You want a title and book cover to catch the eye, dare the prospective reader to flip the book over to find out what it's about.

There is no doubt that a great cover helps sell your book. You should start working on your cover before you finish your novel so you don't feel rushed to finish and get it out before it's the best you can do. On each of my first three novels I wrote the entire book before I started on the cover. Each time I was so exhausted with the project that I just wanted them finished and the cover wasn't as eye catching and good as it should be. I found a talented guy on Upwork.com that lives in Romania, Alex Dumitri, he redid my *Sunshine or Lead* cover and did my *Blanket Immunity* cover. I'm content with my covers, I think each one is better than the last - although my first cover has a special place in my heart because my wife is posing on it.

For self-publishing your book, I have used the Amazon CreateSpace platform to create paperback books and Amazon's KDP to create kindle books. Amazon has merged CreateSpace into KDP. The KDP upload process is straight forward, but can be very overwhelming for both the manuscript and the cover. Barnes & Noble has a self-publish process as well, but I've never used it. The key is to play around a bit with each to see which you may prefer to sign up with.

Please remember, it took x months to write your book, it's okay if it takes x days to get it available for sale. It's better to get it just right, even if it takes a little more time. If you aren't tech savvy at all, or are prone to frustration, there are services you can find where you can pay them to walk you through the process. I haven't used one, but imagine there could be good value in avoiding the headaches to receive help. You can Google "help me self-publish" and find dozens of links. I can't tell you who is good or bad, I'd suggest trying on your own first and if you have trouble, then seek help formatting your book.

Visit KDP or whatever site you will use to see what formats they require for the interior in terms of margins and gutter. They will have a template you can download and use, making it fairly straight forward – but it can also be very frustrating to get it perfect. And you must get your book looking good to get people to buy it.

KDP also has a cover creator you can use for free. I tried it for this book, but found the selection far too limited, so hired Alex from Romania to do this. The cost to create a pretty simple cover like this is a little under one hundred bucks on the low end and up to three hundred on the high end. More involved covers could easily cost five hundred, it will take shopping around on your end.

Provide your cover maker samples of covers of books that you like so they can see your style. Provide as much direction as possible in terms of font, tone, colors, images, etc.

Have patience. Get a proof made. Then review everything in it, including how your cover looks and the entire book looks and feels. Should your font be bigger? Are your chapters separated enough so that it feels like a new chapter? I found it helps to start a new chapter on a new page, and to start the chapter about 1/3 of the way down the page. It makes the reader feel like the chapter is really distinct and doesn't just run together.

When you have a proof copy in your hands, you can compare it to other books and now is not the time to rush to publish – take your time and make any changes you think will help the book. Get a beta reader – someone to read it for the very first time. See how long it takes them to start, to finish, and their thoughts along the way. If they have trouble starting, maybe the book is too long and intimidates them. If they have trouble finishing, find out why – they may have suggestions to make the story more compelling and gripping. Find out why they are or aren't interested in what happens next and see if there are ways you can improve.

You want a story that you know people can read and enjoy before it's officially released for sale. If you have two family members and a friend say they couldn't finish, don't be discouraged, don't argue with them. Ask why. Then see if you can re-work the book to score better with your beta readers. You need to have people read the story and tell you they like it before you can try to sell your novel.

20. Selling Your Book

I would rate this step worse than editing, except for the feeling of pride and joy you get when someone reads your book and enjoys it. The lead character in my first series is Aaron Baker, he was influenced by two of my friends, Aaron Hunter and Matt Baker. I'd never written fiction outside of mandatory creative writing courses in high school and college so when I told Matt about my book he bought it out of loyalty. A week later he called me and said, "I was afraid it was really going to suck. It didn't. It was actually pretty good." That made me feel like I had something. It was my first try, without a professional editor, without the same team behind me that I have now, and it didn't suck. But not sucking isn't going to sell a whole lot of books, even at $3.00.

What I did have was a product I felt I could honestly stand behind to sell at the price point it was offered at. I can stand behind my books and recommend them. That is the standard you have to have. If your book is your first try, without an editor, without a team, then it is really hard to compete with Dan Brown or James Patterson. But they are our competition. So is on-demand television, Netflix, video games, and every book ever published available on instant download – there is a lot of competition.

If you are going to sell your book, you are telling the reader it's worth their money to buy it and their time to read it. To do that, you truly have to believe in it and be honest about its quality. Your market of readers won't finish a book that is too hard to follow, has giant plot holes, isn't compelling, or is riddled with typos and bad grammar – no matter how good your idea and plot are.

If you've taken all the steps I've outlined here to heart, especially the editing, you should have a novel you can stand behind and market with pride. And that's where your sales will come from. You get one person to read it, if they enjoy it, they tell their friends and post on social media about it. If that leads to another sale, then another, you can reach out to a good swath of readers. You can also turbocharge your outreach by paying for advertising on Facebook, on Amazon, or through countless other avenues.

In full disclosure, I haven't spent much time or money marketing, yet. I did a paid book review at onlinebookclub.org for *The Dinosaur Lawyer* that cost me a hundred bucks. I got a 5 out of 5 star review and a series of positive comments about the review, yet that translated into zero book sales.

KDP allows you to track sales quite easily. I did Amazon promotions that put the ad on their shoppers' pages and if they clicked I paid Amazon thirty cents. I had a few dozen clicks, but that led to only one sale. I've spoken at a book store at a local author event which led to seven sales. I've paid for an author booth at a book festival and sold about twenty copies.

The single biggest driver of my sales has been asking people to buy my book in person and on social media. Word of mouth referrals is how I grew my successful law practice – but book sales are not like clients. I couldn't handle a hundred new clients, but could easily handle a hundred new book sales. So this is an area where I'll be looking to expand, starting with social media and I strongly urge you to get ahead of me by establishing your social media presence before you try to sell your book or get it in the hands of an agent.

I have an Amazon author page and recently started a Facebook author page and Instagram page. I may bite the bullet and pay someone for help with a website and marketing to see if I can get return on my investment. Make sure you establish a social media presence as soon as possible.

Since you've made it this far in this book, we're basically friends now and I'll reveal that I am a huge fan of value and am thrifty, i.e., cheap. If you chose my book over more expensive competitors, I totally understand, when I was looking for a book like this I didn't want to pay a lot. In hindsight, buying ten books at ten dollars apiece would have been well worth it. But this is a good lesson for where you should price your novel when you release it.

When you price your book for sale, I suggest the lowest possible price permitted that will not lose you money. Sure, six bucks for your ebook is a great price, but if you bought this book over another because it was a few bucks cheaper, keep that lesson in mind for pricing your own book.

And here's the question for you, did you get the value for whatever you paid for this book? If you're Stephen King, no, this book would be worth nothing to you. If you're an aspiring novelist, did this book help point you in the right direction for how to start and give some pointers for how you can write a better novel? If you are my target market, I believe that you will benefit by reading this book – so I can market and sell this book with pride. And of course, it was reviewed by several people prior to publishing who think there is value in it too.

If your writing group can give you an honest thumbs up, if a few of your friends can give you an honest thumbs up, then you can search for an agent or publish and market your book with pride

If you're getting negative feedback. If you're getting people afraid to read it or tell you about it – don't get discouraged. You need a Travis Lee to come remind you what Hemingway said, "The first draft of anything is shit." It takes a lot of time and effort to turn shit into a coal. It takes more time and effort to produce a rough diamond. And it takes a lot of polish to make a shiny diamond. And it's much easier to sell a diamond than shit.

Whatever novel you have finished on your path should be precious to you. My novels are flawed, even after each chapter averaged five rounds of edits and the entire novel had another five. Meaning each chapter has been looked at ten times by me. Plus by five other people. Yet there are still typos, grammar mistakes, and things I could write better.

Because I listened to input, reworked and improved my novels, I can stand behind them and ask people I meet to give them a try. I submit it's impossible to create a flawless book, that's not your goal. But if you write the steps and produce the best book you can – you will find more success in creating a quality novel and selling it than if you never read this book.

Running The Steps Again

If you're ready. Go write your novel. If you want to do the process again, let's run through all the steps for starting a new novel.

1. Idea – After some good brainstorming I like the idea of a love story set during the American Revolution. The son of a British general falls in love with the daughter of an American soldier.

2. Plot – After some more brainstorming we think of some of the people and major events. Our protagonist is Betsy, a pretty 17 year old girl. She falls in love with Ross, the 18 year old handsome son of a British general. One key plot point, Ross will kill Betsy's little brother on the battlefield, not knowing it was Betsy's brother. Another, Ross asks Betsy to stay at her father's house for safety, she overhears troop movements, and has decide between her love of country and love of Ross. We have a lot of good stuff coming in the general plot, we'll want to build a lot of tension, have it all come to a peak, and then decide if Ross and Betsy stay together or choose their own families.

3. Target Audience – We are going after the Young Adult market, with intentional spillover to the housewife and American History markets. This means we will want to have accurate information for the revolutionary war, we will have to do some research as to what life was like, what cities this type of relationship could happen in, and how plausible the relationship we see developing is. And because we are in the YA market, we want to build up the angst with Ross and Betsy at every turn.

4. Logline – This is tough. It is very tough to focus our novel so early on in the brainstorming process, but let's do our best to see how we want to focus our novel right now. We can always come back to change it later.

Betsy, an American girl found true love with Ross, son of a British general in Boston, during the revolutionary war. Can true love conquer war in this thrilling historical drama?

Honestly, I don't love that logline, but once we write more of the story we will revisit it. Remember, you aren't seeking perfection in your first initial logline.

5.   Storyboard/Outline. We have some of the plot points, so we need to put them into order:

- Betsy and Ross meet, we set the year to 1770 and we have Betsy and Ross meet early in the morning on the day of trial of the Boston Massacre where John Adams famously defended the British soldiers. After the trial, a mob chases Ross because he's in his uniform and she protects him. Maybe she's 14 and he's 15 at the time.

- They engage in letter writing, meeting rarely, but fall deep in love.

- In June of 1774 Ross proposes, Betsy accepts.

- In July of 1774 there is a skirmish where Ross kills Betsy's brother.

- In September of 1774 Ross learns that he killed Betsy's brother.

- In October of 1775 Betsy and Ross get married. Ross never tells about the brother.

- In 1777, Betsy learns Ross killed her brother. That gets her sneaking through papers and she learns of troop movements and wants to get them to General Washington.

- Ross learns of Betsy's plan, and has to choose to defect or turn his pregnant wife in for treason.

The idea is to think about material that will be in chapters and get the events in order. As a writer we have to know the order of our story in order to communicate it effectively to the reader.

6. Character Outline/Development – For Betsy, we're going to pick an emotionally strong woman that we know as a role model for Betsy. We're going to be inspired by the real life person and have Betsy do what we think they would do in these situations. We'll give her a quirk, maybe she always washes her clothes, or hates washing clothes, so when she's doing something in dirty clothes later in the story its funny. We'll stay consistent with her personality throughout the book and make her the kind of person the reader wants to be like.

We'll do the same thing for Ross. We'll imagine what it's like to have a controlling father, have your life planned out for you, and to want that life too – but to maybe want something with Betsy even more. We'll give him a sense of humor that can make Betsy laugh, even in, and especially in, times of stress.

7. Show, Don't Tell. When we write about our characters, we will show Betsy is strong. Here's an example:

Heavy sheets of rain bounced up from puddles in the mud. "Shelly's up ahead?" Betsy called out over the roaring rain to her little brother.

George nodded, pointing to the fence ahead. Lightning cracked off in the distance, the ground shook a second later.

"Go back to the house!" Betsy yelled.

George shook his head.

"Now!" Betsy commanded, her eyes reflected another flash of lightning.

Betsy watched George's little feet plop through the mud towards the house before trudging her way to the fence.

Where is that little guy? She tried to block the rain from her eyes with her hands as she scanned water rushing down the trench under the fence. *There.* Betsy noticed the water was running off wider than the other fence posts.

She fought the mud and knelt at the fence. Her stomach turned when she saw the lamb's head under the gushing water.

She plunged her hands into the warm rainwater and pulled the lamb's head to air, it bleated. Betsy put the lamb's head against her chest, seized the creature's chest and pulled.

The lamb bleated in pain and didn't budge free. Its leg was stuck. Betsy's left hand followed the leg under the water and groaned. The heavy trough slid down and crushed the lamb's leg.

Betsy held the lamb's head up and looked at the trough. *What did Archimedes say? Give me a lever long enough and a fulcrum on which to place it, and I shall move the world."*

-- So you can see where this is going, she goes and gets a metal bar or something and frees the little lamb.

We show that Betsy is smart, capable, and cares for people. The reader can conclude that from how Betsy saves the life of the little lamb. We show, we don't tell. This makes the little brother happy and this is the little brother that Ross later kills. We set things up for future plot points.

8. Use Dialogue Effectively. We want to communicate information, entertain the reader, and bring them into the scene.

"There!" Betsy pointed to a barrel. "Put your jacket in there."

"Wha?" Ross gasped out, panic in his eyes.

"Hurry. I'll help you." Betsy looked down the street, no sign of the pursuers yet.

With the grace of a wildebeest stuck in a straightjacket, Ross ripped at his buttons and removed his heavy red military coat, shoving it into the barrel to which Betsy held the lid.

Betsy put the lid on the barrel, she could hear the ruckus coming. "Help me up there." Betsy pushed up to sit on top of the barrel.

"We're not running?" Ross asked, fear dripping from his voice.

"Kiss me." She could hear the crowd coming. "Now."

Ross put her arms around her waist. She grabbed his head with her hands, mussing his hair as she kissed him.

Nearly a dozen boys and men hustled towards them. The tallest one in the group shouted, "You see a Brit come through here?"

Betsy pulled back from Ross and pointed down the street. "Just a second ago, a red coat ran there."

You can see how the dialogue is woven into the story, it makes you feel like you're in the moment. When things calm down, we'll have Ross thank her – they can recap what happened, tell jokes, etc.

9. Find Your Character's Voice. We'll make Betsy self-educated. Very bright, but not polished or refined. She's going to constantly be in that voice. She's not going to swear, but she's also not going to sound stuffy. She's a pretty easy voice to capture and will naturally say the wrong thing from time to time in front of Ross' family – which will up her angst and tension.

10. Do Not Shift View Points Willy-Nilly. During the little chase and kiss scene, we were in Betsy's head the entire time, we didn't jump from Ross' head then back to Betsy's. We stuck in her point of view the entire time. We will stick to being in one person's head per chapter or scene break, or clearly signal to the reader we are switching heads by using an object as a transition.

11. Chapter Length. We'll keep the first chapter length to 1500 words or so, then each chapter thereafter will average about 2500.

12. Novel Length. Depending on how much history we want to go into, this seems like a Young Adult novel, probably shoot for about 65,000 words, as low as 60 and high as 75.

13. Determine Our Ending. We plan on having Betsy and Ross married, raising a family together in the United States. To get there, we'll want a lot of tension and entertainment.

14. Climaxes are Important. The story will build to the point where Betsy, six months pregnant and married to Ross learns that Ross killed her beloved little brother. Betsy then learns secretes of the British army that would help her country, Ross discovers this and the two have only a moment to decide their fate because a soldier suspects Betsy of disloyalty. Everything comes to ahead when Ross tells her to throw the troop plans into the fireplace and kisses her like nothing's wrong just as a soldier suspecting her of taking the plans approaches. Kind of a circle back to how Betsy saved Ross from the Americans. Then Ross will redraw the plans from his memory and deliver them to the American army when he defects.

15. Inciting Incidents. Remembering the goal of our novels are to make the reader want to turn the page – the way we do that is to have specific incidents that the reader wants to know how they resolve. Since this is a love story, we'll start with Betsy and Ross meeting at a market in the morning before the big trial, both going for the last loaf of bread. We'll be in Betsy's POV and her heart will flutter, she'll be so angry he took the bread, but so surprised when he runs up to her to give her the loaf like a gentleman. Since this was an era with no cell phones, we get them to make plans to see each other that night. Because this isn't a shooting or chase, we really have to put the reader into the scene, have them understand the longing, aching, and desire that Betsy has. Make them want to turn the page to find out what happens between Betsy and Ross.

16. Find Your Story Pacing. Because the climax of the story is Betsy's decision to choose country over Ross, and Ross choosing Betsy of country, we will spend more time focusing on characters than plot points in the story. For this type of story we can and should do a chapter explaining that Betsy's father didn't teach her to read, treated her like a second class citizen. But Betsy loved to learn, she would eavesdrop on her little brother's lessons, one of which was when she learned about Archimedes statement about the fulcrum and lever. Betsy's eavesdropping for schooling could be done while doing laundry – hence her love of laundry.

Maybe little brother knew, helped teach Betsy how to read and write and went out of his way for Betsy to overhear his lessons. This could be very compelling background information to help the reader get to know, understand, and appreciate Betsy. We probably don't want to spend four chapters on the school lessons, but a chapter touching on it would be perfect to keep the reader engaged and wanting to find out what happens next. Plus this is a great way to tie in various parts of the story and it's always rewarding when the story revisits something told earlier.

17. Telling and Finishing Your Story. Why did I use this example? Two reasons, when my wife proofreads it, I think she'll enjoy it. And second, to show you that the steps in this book work for either a thriller or an angsty love story. Make sure you tell the story you want and finish it accordingly.

18. Submitting Your Manuscript to an Agent. Let's circle back – we've just finished our first chapter. We submit that to a writing group or to a fellow author to trade reviews. We give them no more than 3000 words because people will be more willing to read one chapter than an entire book. If they have suggestions, we listen with an open mind, we think about or plot, our logline, and we move forward with our writing with knowledge that all stories can be improved. We give pieces at a time for editing, we do not wait until we finish an entire first draft then hand someone a three hundred page draft and ask for their help editing it. We edit along the way.

When the manuscript has been fully edited, each chapter has had your eyes review it ten times, and you've had at least three other people read it – then you can submit it to an agent. Also, we will do a search for writing competitions in our genre, see if we can find any for free, or any that seem reputable at a reasonable cost. You have to do your own legwork to find competitions to enter, the effort is worth it as they can be a good way to get a stamp of approval on your novel.

19. Creating Your Book. On the cover, I see Betsy and Ross holding hands, hands almost disconnecting because they are being pulled apart. There's a faded out cannon in the background, maybe the Betsy Ross American flag (in your novel, please come up with more original names than Pro, Crush, Betsy and Ross for your characters. Also, don't have Mary, Marty, Mark and Markus as your characters – use different first letters and different length names to make your story easier to read.) I'd pick a font like Bookman Old Style or Garamond. Something with a little bit more flare than Times New Roman, but still classic and easy to read.

For a title, *Revolutionary Love*. People often hear revolutionary and think war, love is the opposite. It's short, cute, but maybe too cute. Some alternatives: *America's First Love Story, The Tale of Betsy Stone, Betsy's Tale*. We'd workshop the titles with friends, see what's catchy, then choose what we like best.

20. Selling Your Book. Let's say we self-publish and we entered a few writing contests (found by doing a Google search for writing contests and spending an hour sorting through various competitions). We also need to get the book into hands of people who will read it and post reviews. There are two kinds of review. Editorial reviews where you can try to get your local newspaper to write one of your book, or pay for Kirkus, Onlinebookclub, or numerous others. Editorial reviews are good and so are customer reviews. A mix of both is ideal, with customer reviews being more important. The problem is, when so many friends provide reviews for independent authors, it's hard to trust the review. That's why it's important to get many reviews. Once ten, then twenty reviews are posted, potential purchases will believe the reviews are less likely to be biased friends and family members posting and the reviews will be more trusted.

Think of how many books you've read. Think of how many times you've written a book review. Getting one review for every twenty people who read your book is a reasonable goal.

Now think about when you look at a book or anything else at Amazon for purchase, you probably like to see at least twenty customer reviews before you are comfortable making the purchase. Keep that in mind, be patient gathering reviews, respectfully ask people to review your book for you – and understand not everyone who reads it will give it 5 stars.

Once you have a bunch of favorable reviews, let social media know about them. Find independent local bookstores and ask if they have a local author event where you can come in to sell and sign books. Ask people you meet if they would take a look at your book. Ask people who reviewed your book positively to post to their own social media about it. Basically, get out and promote yourself. You worked the steps, you followed the path, you have a novel you can be proud of – you can respectfully ask people to buy it.

CONCLUSION

You understand the five parts of a novelist's path and have twenty steps to finish your novel. When you publish your novel, find me (Adam Van Susteren) on social media and let me know. If you can't find me, make sure you do a better job with your online presence so that people can actually find you. How else can someone ask you to come speak to their book club or find out information on your next book? Please do message me, I honestly would like to hear if my tips helped you or not and would like to hear about the novel you've finished.

If you finished reading this book, please put up an honest review on Amazon or wherever you review books like these. Honest reviews are critical for the future success of our industry. If this book was only 1, 2, or 3 stars for you, explain why in your review. If you already knew the information or disagree with some of the information presented, it may help a prospective reader understand why they may, or may not, like this book.

Like all books, this one is not intended for everyone. The goal is to help lay out the path and inspire aspiring authors to write and edit a novel that they can be proud of. Well-written stories will always in demand. I want you to take that first step and think of your idea then take twenty steps down the path: write, read, review, edit and market!

Thank You and Good Luck!